Vanilla Milk
a memoir told in poems
by Chanel Brenner

"The poems inside of this book were torn from the heart of a woman whose suffering is so immense that it could swallow her whole. Instead of letting the staggering pain consume her, Chanel Brenner crafted these undeniably gorgeous meditations on the death of her son. I read *Vanilla Milk* four times before putting it down, because I was afraid to let it go. Chanel Brenner has crafted a resplendent work of art that is unrivaled in its ability to make sense of the ebbs and flows of grief."

        MATTHEW LOGELIN
        New York Times bestselling author of *Two Kisses for Maddy*

"Chanel Brenner's *Vanilla Milk* is a transcendent work. The skill and courage of these poems inspires me to be a better writer, the generosity in them inspires me to be a better person."

        MIA SARA
        author at [PANK] Magazine

"Brenner's book joins the ranks of great elegies or lamentations for the loss of a child: Ben Jonson's poem for his son, Jan Kochanowski's *Laments*, Stephane Mallarme's unfinished long poem "A Touch of Anatole," and two contemporary works—Stan Rice's *Some Lamb* and Edward Hirsch's *Gabriel*. Brenner's book of poems dealing with the loss of her son Riley stands along with these great classics—art's attempt through poetry to fathom the unfathomable sorrow of suffering. *Vanilla Milk* breaks the heart, moves the soul as few books of poetry can—but, like all great art, it heals as well. You will never see the world the same way again."

        JACK GRAPES
        author of *The Naked Eye, Method Writing,* and *Poems So Far So Far So Good So Far to Go*

Vanilla Milk

Vanilla Milk
a memoir told in poems

Chanel Brenner

SILVER BIRCH PRESS
LOS ANGELES, CALIFORNIA

Copyright 2014, Chanel Brenner, ALL RIGHTS RESERVED

ISBN-13: 978-0692267479

ISBN-10: 0692267476

FIRST EDITION: October 2014

Email: silver@silverbirchpress.com

Web: silverbirchpress.com

Blog: silverbirchpress.wordpress.com

Mailing Address:
Silver Birch Press
P.O. Box 29458
Los Angeles, CA 90029

For Riley

Preface

The night Riley died, I sat down at my computer and started to write a poem. It was only the fifth poem I had ever written. It was not good. But writing it was. Thinking about the words, the placement of words, controlling the words.

I read and wrote. I carried my journal with me everywhere. I wrote poems at stoplights in the car, in the grocery store, waiting in line at the post office. Instead of crying, I wrote poems. A lot of poems. When someone asked me how many children I had, I wrote a poem. When I ran into Riley's best friend at the market, I wrote a poem. When I saw a woman with a child at Target slumped over in a wheelchair with a breathing tube, I wrote a poem. When Riley's brother, Desmond, asked, "Why did Riley die?" I wrote a poem. When Geoffrey the giraffe from Toys 'R' Us left a birthday message for Riley and added, "Can you believe you are another year older?" on our answering machine, I wrote a poem.

I have never been much of a crier, but the death of my son didn't leave me a choice. The pain had to go somewhere. Writing poems about my dead son was so much better than crying. I didn't get a stuffy nose. I didn't feel exhausted. I didn't get puffy raccoon eyes. No wasted Kleenex. No lost tears. No lost time. Instead, I gained something: my thoughts on paper. Words arranged in a specific order. Something to honor Riley. Something to keep him alive.

Contents

I.

The Perfect Latch / 17
Toy Venom / 18
Shifting Sand / 19
Choices / 20
The Robot Poet / 22
A Moment of Chaos / 23
Your Permanent Tooth / 24
Happy Hour / 25
Blindsided / 26
Something Else / 27
Not Riley / 28
Safe / 29

II.

Mothering My Son's Dead Brother / 33
Knowing / 34
The Trip / 35
Back to the Future / 36
I Have 2x the Love for 1 Child / 37
The Give Away / 38
I Want / 39
Out of Body / 40
Where the World Ends / 41
Fucking Rite Aid / 42
The Four Corners / 43
Only One / 44
It Is Morning In the Kitchen / 45
Riley's Rosebush / 46
What Would Wislawa Szymborska Do? / 47
Riley Died Again Yesterday / 48

III.

Mothering a Dead Child / 53
Enough / 54
The Birthday Party / 55
I Miss My Son / 56
Out of Order / 57
Keeping the Dead / 58
Into the Schoolyard / 59
A Break / 60
When a Friend Asks What I've Done with Riley's Clothes / 61
Can't Imagine / 62
Riley Day / 63
Catching Up / 65
What We Carry / 66
What Remains / 67

IV.

My Friend from Another Life / 71
Vanilla Milk / 72
Super Boy / 73
God as a Waiter / 75
July 28th, 2012 / 76
I Read Somewhere Only Ten Percent of Marriages Survive the
    Death of a Child / 77
Heaven / 78
Somethin' New Is Brewin' / 79
The Unlearning / 80
The Perfect Kiss / 81
His Heart Takes Flight / 82

Family Photos / 85-101

Acknowledgments / 103
About the Author / 104

Vanilla Milk

I

The Perfect Latch

She didn't expect breastfeeding
to be so difficult—temples
throbbing, her body tense.
She's not who she expected to be,
not who she was or will become.
Nipples raw and cracked,
burning like resentment,
she squeezes her left breast
to achieve the perfect latch.

She feeds, bathes, changes—
despite her mistakes,
and frustration, impatience,
and lost temper, despite
every imperfection—
the child loves back.

Toy Venom

The boy was so excited he shrieked, "yippee," and flung his head from side to side so hard his mother worried he'd injure himself as they unwrapped the toy. Surprised by the length and sharpness of the creature's tongue, she forbade him to sleep with it, so he made a bed on the floor with a pillow and blanket for the action figure. When he awoke during the night, he climbed down and fell asleep with it.

This morning, while applying lotion to her legs, she hears the doorknob squeak before she sees him squinting in the sunlight. "Mommy, my nose hurts," he says, as she continues applying lotion.

He complains as much as she did at his age, so much, her father allotted five minutes once a day for her complaining. According to him, she used every second.

She wore a white hat towel on her head, her son's name for it. "Do you like my hat?," she would ask. "I do not like your hat," he'd reply. Now, when she asks, he stands silent, pale and scrunched. If she'd looked closely, she'd have noticed the change in his face.

"Mommy, my nose really hurts. It hurts so bad I can't stand it." Now she reaches for him.

"What happened?"

"Toy Venom's tongue went up my nose. I slept with him on the floor. I'm sorry."

"I told you not to. Let me take a look." She peers into his nostrils and sees healthy pink flesh. "It looks okay," she soothes. "The nose is very sensitive, that's probably why it hurts so much. Let's go get some orange juice, that should help."

While she's making breakfast, a peculiar sound emanates from the living room where he's drinking his juice. She sees him throw up, his body convulsing. When it stops, he lies on the floor near the pool of orange foam and says he wants to sleep. His eyes close. She shakes him. He wakes for a second, then passes out.

Terror runs her to his bedroom—sharp tongue-brain damage-toxic plastic-lead-yesterday flailing head-her fault-hospital *now*—she grabs Venom for the doctor, who'll say the problem is not the toy.

Shifting Sand

I sit beside my son's
hospital bed.
The fluorescent lights are so bright
I don't know how he sleeps,
but he does.
His father paces the hallway,
still in his suit jacket,
phone to his ear.
When I shift my foot, I feel sand
between the linoleum
and the sole of my shoe.
Yesterday, my son swung
and jumped like Superman,
landed in the safety of the playground.
After school, I shook the sand
from his shoes on our front porch, annoyed
by how it seemed never-ending.
Now, his blue Nikes
lie between me and the bed,
sand spilling out.
I shift my foot, grinding the finite grains
against the scarred linoleum,
to the rhythm of his breathing.

Choices

The nurse places two boxes of tissue, a cheery pink water pitcher, saltines, and an apple juice container resembling a child's oversized juice box on the long table. She peers beyond us in the coffin-shaped room designated for PICU visitors. Laughter expels from me like lava. This is how they handle parents of a dying child, where they hide the grief.

My laugh surprises a chuckle from the nurse that sticks in the wrong pipe. She covers her mouth at the sound, exiting as if she'd disturbed a memorial service.

I memorize items as if studying for a final exam. Tissue box, six inches from the ten-inch-high juice box, three inches from the sweating water pitcher, and the pregnant puddle around its base. I nibble a cracker that clumps like ash on my tongue.

The doctors file in like pallbearers, heads bent, eyes averted, sitting at the table's end, like a fading crescent moon. All but one stare at their clipboards and paper, while their leader speaks, words dropped like stones on tile floor, "If he was eighty, we'd let nature take its course, but because he's a child, we're offering you choices:

One: We do nothing and your child dies.

Two: We cut a hole in his skull to drain the blood and relieve the pressure, but he'll likely still die.

Three: We remove the clot, but he'll probably die on the operating table or shortly after. If he survives he'll most likely never talk, understand or walk, breathe or eat, and we still can't remove the AVM.

Four: We do an angiogram and gather more information about the extent of the damage, and then make a decision. We'll still put the tube in, drain the blood if possible, then perform one, two, or three, depending."

The fluorescent lights flicker insistently as we ask the doctor to repeat the choices. His words hang in the air like volcanic smoke and ash, as I remember my mother's advice just days ago about an insignificant decision, "Do whatever you want. That's the great thing about life, we have choices." My head cranes up to meet the flickering, the room quiet except for a baby's wailing, muffled by the layers of drywall, wood, and insulation dividing us; I think of our son's body down the hall, beyond successive layers of God knows what.

The Robot Poet

Riley and Szymborska meet in the meadow,
outside the gold pyramid and wizard's cave.
Hi, I'm Riley. I make robots.
His eyes are serious, handshake firm.
Hi, I'm Wislawa. I write poems.
They sit side by side,
writing and making a robot.
She writes of a boy with hair and eyes
the color of earth,
of his steadfast concentration
as he creates a robot in her likeness.
He assembles a mechanical body
from intricately ordered words,
his vocabulary now boundless.
They work for hours, or days,
or less than a second.
I can't say with certainty;
Death makes time
too vast to measure.
The sun never sets,
the wildflowers bloom forever.
The double rainbow stretches
for eternity in the cloudless sky.

A Moment of Chaos

The Wednesday before Riley died, my two boys were up to their usual antics, bouncing at the table, knees on chairs, arms flailing, chanting, "Me first! Me first! Me first!" as I prepared dinner.

Our house in its usual end-of-day state, toys tornadoed around the room, fragments of paper and cardboard, the always-empty tape dispenser gracing the kitchen floor.

They had dinner guests, Riley's robots in chairs next to them, bodies made from empty five-gallon water bottles, waffle box heads, and swimming-goggle eyes, dressed in cast-off clothes and hats, empty plates waiting.

I microwaved Riley's second-favorite (and easier), meal, tortillas with canned beans and grated cheese. I'd like to say that I did this with ease, enjoying the evening with my boys, instead of thinking, "I'm not cut out for this shit. Who was I to think I could raise two boys? I was the girl who developed an eye twitch dating a slightly hyper man." I had a full bladder. I was hungry, thirsty, my chest tight, my heart racing, chaos getting the best of me, when a thought stopped me, I would miss the chaos when my teenagers retreated to shut bedrooms. I inhaled slowly and focused on my boys' beautiful, flailing bodies, on their smiles and glowing skin—I took a long moment to breathe them in.

Your Permanent Tooth

When I brush your brother's teeth,
I think of the last night I brushed
your big, brand-new front tooth.

We waited so long for it,
three years of your trademark
toothless smile's jagged edge.

Evidence of my carelessness
when you were three,
and I chased you from the bath,

wrapped in your giraffe's-head
hooded towel, playing tickle-mommy,
running and laughing till you fell—

dentist confirming what I knew:
you'd lose both front teeth early,
my first loss of you,

but only baby teeth, not permanent.
Funny we called it permanent,
you only had it for a week.

Happy Hour

En route to a wedding reception,
my husband says, *I think our wedding
could have been more serious.*

I thought the same thing, listening
to their traditional vows, *in sickness
and health, in good times and bad,*
the bride and groom's forty-something
faces heavy with the time it took
to find each other.

Just barely thirty,
we laughed through
our vows, like teenagers
at their prom.

The judge, not rabbi,
relayed stories we told him
about our relationship,
nachos eaten with knife and fork,
and how to get the last
Tic-Tac from the container
without slamming it on
the nearest hard surface.

Our vows consisted of promises
like sleeping by each other's side
and laughing together.

We offered ourselves to each other
lightly as happy hour hors d'oeuvres.

I think about the vows
we'd make today
and wonder if a dead child
rests in the clause
until death do us part.

Blindsided

I found the surprise

you left for me

in my journal,

eating at your favorite restaurant,

the place with cheesy eggs

and heart-shaped cookies,

your name written backwards

yelir, a trident for a Y,

and a picture you drew

of yourself, right arm raised

as if to say goodbye or hello.

Something Else

You were never still,

your feet barely

touched the ground.

You floated, changed shape,

moved unpredictably.

Sometimes, I feared you would

just float away.

What are you now?

A flicker of light,

an unexpected surge of water,

a false alarm?

I look up to see you,

but not through my eyes,

and time dissolves

like the gravity of two worlds

has pulled it together

and we are something else.

Not Riley

We walk by foods you loved,
vanilla milk you chanted for,
and your brother after you,
banilla, banilla, banilla.
Now, he wants chocolate
I don't feel right buying.
Earlier, he asked about the potholder
you wove in school, and I told him
he could make one too.
He looked at me with his blue,
not brown, eyes, and said clearly,
I'm Desmond. Not Riley.

Safe

When our alarm blares at four a.m., I forget,
waiting for you to run to me for comfort.

I yell to wake your father,
you know how deep he sleeps.

He lurches from bed ready to fight,
but needs to find his glasses.

Once, I would have assumed
it was a false alarm,

told you why you were safe
in your bed, bedroom and house,

but safe has lost all meaning.
Your father checks windows and doors for me

like he would have done for you.
I hold your Mickey Mouse doll

and pretend to feel safe
like you would have done for me.

II

Mothering My Son's Dead Brother

While strapping Desmond
into his car seat he asks,
Mommy, where did you go?

What do you mean?, I deny.

I forgot to strap Riley
into his car seat once
and drove five blocks—

till he yelled,
You forgot to strap me in!

I want Desmond to play outside
like his brother did,
but he doesn't want to.

I don't like to get dirty,
he reminds me.

Desmond gets a rash
when I get lost writing
and forget to hydrate
his sensitive skin.

You were gone a really long time,
he says, and his knowing
brings me home.

Knowing

My husband asks me during dinner,
if I'd marry him again,
knowing what I know now.
I give the question the time
it deserves, an honest pause,
study my Loup de Mer,
sip my Prosecco,
before telling the man facing me,
this time seated
instead of on bended knee.
I answer, *yes*, and he says,
You must be a masochist.

The Trip

When I think of all I did to protect my son,
all I worried he could die from:
suffocation, cancer,
accidents, poison—
all distractions
from the actual,
his destiny at rest
in its recliner
biding time,
death in his head
like a landmine waiting.

Back to the Future

Your father wants to know

if we could have saved you.

He's hunched over the computer

nightly, reading AVM websites,

sure he'll find a cure.

I say, *We can't go back,*

but your father wants an answer.

I ask him, *When you find it, then what?*

You know what he tells me?

He'll invent a time machine.

I Have 2x the Love for 1 Child

Since the death
of my older son,

I worry that the weight
of my love is too heavy.

I see my son hunched over,
carrying my grief

like a load of stones.
I worry he'll learn

to bask in that love
till he sunburns,

come to crave
the sting and heat of it.

I worry that he is forming
like a rock in a river bed,

my grief-ridden love
rushing over him

like whitewater.
I worry that one day,

a woman will ask him
why her love is not enough,

and he won't know
the answer.

The Give Away

Nothing belongs to us, not our hair, not our thoughts,
not our sons.

Doctor wearing white cowboy boots scuffed with death says,
Cash in your chips.

The birds sing their undying tune.

A washing machine outlives a little boy.

These are the ruins: hair, eyes, teeth, flesh over bones.

What parts of his body do we want to give away?

Not his eyes, they matched his hair perfectly.

I Want

I changed my mind:

I want my son back.

I want his donated

heart and liver back.

I want his kidneys.

I even want

his arteriovenous

malformation back.

I want his body back

unharmed, un-burned.

I want him buried

in a proper casket,

uncut, intact.

I want, I want, I want—

Out of Body

My therapist says,
Do the things that make you happy,
even if they don't anymore.
I go to lunch with a friend,
order champagne,
but while eating Steelhead and salad,
I feel disconnected from my body.
My friend, holding her chalice
of sparkling water, confides
she's pregnant.
I say I'm happy for her, and I am.
Not happy like I would have been
if my son were alive, but happy
enough to toast her with champagne,
while I float
above myself like a bubble,
staring at the gutted
fish on my plate.

Where the World Ends

My four-year-old
wants the world flat,
unnerved by
this hurtling ball
we live on.
He wants to run
right to the edge—
see where it ends.
I agree,
life should provide
clear signage:
End of the World,
Heaven This Way,
Escape Exit Here.
My son shouldn't
have to answer
whether he has
a brother or sister,
shouldn't have
to whisper,
I had a brother.

Fucking Rite-Aid

I saw a toy you would have loved,

from that weird show you liked,

Phinneas and Ferb.

You'd lie on the couch, like your father,

laughing hysterically.

We didn't let you watch much TV,

but after your first hospital stay

when you endured more than most adults,

we let you watch all you wanted.

I picked the toy up and put it back,

the last of its kind.

I keep wondering if someone else

has bought it, and stopping myself

from going back.

The Four Corners

Desmond leaves his seat, plops himself down in the vacant fourth chair at our table. "Why is there another chair?" He slouches in the seat as if slipping his foot into a shoe too big for him. His eyes scan the restaurant as if he expects someone, then retreat inward, and far away. A plate of half-eaten quesadilla, beans and rice wait on the table in front of his abandoned chair.

We meet Desmond's question with a pause and a glance of kindred spirit before I explain, "All the tables this size have four chairs, look around us." My son looks around the mostly empty room and nods, but the unspoken truth hovers like a helicopter close to peril. Our fourth chair is not insignificant like the ones at the other tables, and he knows it. It is his brother's chair he's usurped, and part of me wants him out of it, as if he sits on top of his brother's absence.

Only One

Is he your only child?
You only have one? Yes, one,
only, only, only one.
Only-lonely-one.
I used to have two,
now only one,
I want to say.
One died,
I don't want to say.
Two, and then one.
Only-lonely-one.
Some little boys don't grow up.
That's not always what they do.
Some disappear,
growth stunted
forever at size six,
reduced to forty-four
cubic inches, the size
of the urn.
Only one. Only, only, only one.
Only-lonely-one.

It Is Morning in the Kitchen

When Desmond asks me,
Who is Riley?, swinging
his three-year-old legs,
facing away from me,

separate in our grief
for my other son,
like two children swinging
out of sync, passing
with opposite trajectories.

His question
knocks me off
my swing,
and fills my mouth with sand,

preventing me
from speaking.

Riley's Rosebush

The bush has more buds

than any other year,

extravagant red blooming.

The Wednesday before Riley died,

he wanted to cut some for me,

but they weren't ready yet.

The Wednesday after,

I cut them for myself,

placed them in a plastic cup

with too much water,

then plopped them on

our kitchen table.

What Would Wislawa Szymborska Do?

Un-burn his flesh, return chips
of bone and teeth, powdery ashes,
like seeds in soil newly sown.

Reclaim his heart,
kidneys, liver, kindly return
the recipients their own.

Cross a line through the words,
He died, reclassify
Arteriovenous Malformation,
a work of fiction.

Tuck him back in his bed
to awaken from dreaming.

Create something out
of nothing, life from loss.
Isn't that what poets do?

Riley Died Again Yesterday

We ordered food from a place
we used to get delivery, before.
The doorbell rings and there she is,
glowing and smiling like always.
How are your two boys?

Desmond stands, close, so like his brother,
you could mistake him if you squinted.
My hand on his head, I tell her Riley died.

She goes dark as a sudden cloud,
hand over her mouth as she sobs,
she says, *I'm so sorry* too many times to stand.

I hug her,
and say it's okay,
he was a beautiful boy,
and we miss him,
my arm wet with her tears.

She says she was excited
to see our order, to enjoy his running,
hug, and Spider-Man stories.

She says, *My cancer came back,
and almost got me.*
I picture the last time they saw each other,
Death's finger pointing,
Eeny, meeny, miny, moe.

III

Mothering a Dead Child

I can't stop writing poems
about my dead son.
He's why I started,
and I worry I won't
be able to stop.
I'm afraid of trapping
his spirit.
I like to think
I keep him alive,
but can't know.
I've found no
classes to take
or books to read
explaining how
to mother
a dead child.
What if I'm
overprotective,
boarding up
his bedroom windows,
locking the door,
keeping him for myself,
torturing him
with my poems?
How will I know?
Who will tell me?
How will I stop?

Enough

Desmond stands on his bed,
hugging both of us at once,
stretching his small arms'
whole length, as if
there's not enough of him
to meet our needs.

More hugs and kisses,
more noise and chaos,
more requests for stories.

He knows his limitations:
two arms, two legs;
three years, not seven,
Desmond, not Riley,
alive, not memorialized.

After the hug, he kisses
each of our cheeks,
until he thinks
we've had enough.

The Birthday Party

We stand on a hilltop at the edge of an expansive, grassy field resembling an unborn cemetery in search of its first headstone. I hold my breath as my son runs down, surrendering his body to gravity's speed. He rolls to a stop at the bottom, splayed like a yard sale. I exhale only as he stands up laughing and runs off to play.

We are picnicking to celebrate Riley's best friend Jacquelle's seventh birthday, with lunch, balloons and cake, with the parents of children Riley would have been in first grade with—and of course—their vibrant children, the age Riley would have been this year.

Riley last saw Jacquelle the Thursday before he died. Her mom and I talked about how they reminded us of an old married couple, with Riley being the high-maintenance one. "Jacquelle, help me with this. Jacquelle, bring me that. Jacquelle, Jacquelle!" until Riley ran into the room upset. He stood between my seated legs, head tilted down, eyes up, "Jacquelle pulled down my pants and saw my privates. I'm so embarrassed!" He buried his face against me as if I were a tortoise shell, while I struggled to keep from laughing, mouth closed tightly as a baby's refusing food.

My husband and I came to honor Riley, though I don't know if he'd approve if he could see us. Sometimes I think I see Riley shining through his brother, as if some energy transferred to Desmond.

Jaquelle's strong voice breaks my thoughts, "Desi! Desi! Desi!," as she races downhill after him. He stops for her, and she bestows one of her famous full-bodied, no-holds-barred hugs that Riley had succumbed to reluctantly at Desmond's age, but eventually came to love. Desmond, however, gives it right back with his whole body, the two of them holding on like long-lost friends from a previous life, and I see Riley's spirit lighting their embrace, feeling, for a moment, as if we belong here.

I Miss My Son

His hands, his eyes,
his sweet, high-pitched voice,

his overuse of Scotch tape,
his out-of-sync kisses.

I miss him calling me, *My Mommy.*
I miss watching him fall asleep,

his eyes fluttering, closing,
popping open again, before finally shutting.

I miss him holding my hand
or walking ahead of me.

I miss his laugh,
its joyous, limitless energy.

I miss his questions I couldn't answer,
Mommy, are we born again?

Out of Order

Desmond says he wants me to have a baby in my tummy, but he wants it born as a big boy, like Riley, for him to play with. I tell him it doesn't work that way.

He asks, "Why Mommy?"

The three of us wait at a stoplight, my husband's hands tense on the steering wheel, his body rigid, his expression withholding and sad. He wears a black shirt, a new color he added to his wardrobe. Because Desmond likes to drive in silence these days, and orders the music off, we obey. He tells us to stop talking, and we shut up. We orbit him like two of Jupiter's moons.

My new dark sense of humor elicits a hollow laugh I don't recognize as mine. Riley's death has scooped a hole in me so deep I can't climb out.

When the light changes, Desmond points to a green space in the city, and yells, "I want to go there!" I refuse, "No, Honey, you don't want to go there, it's a cemetery," but his father obliges, "You will someday."

Keeping the Dead

I.

Desmond finds a hummingbird
on our front porch,
kneels over its stillness.

I don't want to bury it in the dirt, he says.

II.

He wants to put it in a box,
keep it in his room,
take care of it

forever, he says.

III.

At night:
Mommy, is Riley with me?

I think of his brother's clothes
resting in the drawers below his bed,
their little carcasses all lined up.

Into the Schoolyard

He heads the train
of children linked by hands
and lunch baskets,
teacher for a caboose.

I watch from the gate,
waiting for his face,
blond hair curled
from napping, to see me.

I stare shamelessly,
while he's unaware,
astonished by his beauty,
each time like the first,

as if there were something
temporary about his presence
since we lost his older brother,
as if he might flicker and burn out.

When he sees me,
his body picks up speed,
not letting go of the child's hand—

propelling the whole train—
unstoppable in his will
as he breaks free into my arms.

A Break

"Excuse me, doesn't your son take Krav Maga?" I stand, latte in one hand, bowl of avocado and grapefruit in the other, seeking a table. Brown eyes, brown hair, big smile, she seems like a photo I have stumbled on, and any appropriate response abandons me.

I picture Riley in his gray Krav Maga T-shirt and black workout pants, tennis shoes with knotted laces. His serious fighting stance. His spiky, rumpled hair.

"Yes," I finally say, to this woman I hardly know. "Riley. He used to do Krav Maga."

"My daughter's been taking a break too," she says. Her light-hearted words sting like a paper cut. I know I should walk away, leave her believing my son is playing another sport, but I lean close to confide, "I feel like I have to tell you the truth: my son died eight months ago." I force a breath and try to mention Desmond, but our connection's broken. I see damage reflected in her eyes as she stumbles over something—*sorry*.

When a Friend Asks What I've Done with Riley's Clothes

Obviously, something should be done.
His clothes should not hang,
limp and useless as crippled limbs
or hidden in drawers, untouched.
To whom should I surrender the blue shark t-shirt
he wore on his sixth birthday?
Or his favorite orange pullover,
the collar frayed from his daily chewing?
Or the charcoal-gray sweater he wore
eating his last bowl of vanilla ice cream
the night he died?
What should be done?
Nothing, I say, *We haven't done a thing.*

Can't Imagine

Did you know her son died?

    I can hear you.

How are you really doing?

    You don't want the real answer.

Jonathon is ten. Can you believe it?

    No, I can't, but not in the way you can't.

I've been thinking of you.

    Then don't avoid me.

I don't know how you're even standing.

    I didn't lose my legs.

I can't worry about everything I say.

    Neither can I.

I'm writing my daughter off.

    Picture her dead.

Riley Day

It's been almost a year since Riley died, and our azaleas are blooming. Last year when they bloomed, Riley snuck out the door to stand behind me, while I stretched my legs, before my walk. He'd hide silently, enjoying his secret till I discovered him, then laugh uncontrollably.

Sometimes I still turn around. Sometimes I forget, sometimes I pretend. Last year, he wanted to pick roses for me, but they weren't ready. This year, a single red rose blooms on an aberrant branch. I keep wanting to pick it, but don't, not wanting to hasten its life span. Last year, Riley lingered taking down the Valentine's Day decorations all over our house, arranging red hearts, red napkins and plates in the box I brought him. He liked taking them down as much as putting them up. He liked organizing, liked the house being clean, "like a hotel", he said.

"What's next, Mommy? What holiday comes next?" he asked, patting a heart into place. Late afternoon sun splintered our living room's narrow windows as I trudged by to do even more laundry, load number five. It was Sunday, need I say more? Desmond building Lego towers and knocking them down, while his father took his second nap. Did I mention it was Sunday? Feeling grateful Riley removed the Valentines, I noticed the Halloween and Christmas decorations still sitting on the side porch. He'd been bugging his dad for weeks to put them in the garage. In a hurry to do more laundry, get more shit done, I knew Riley wanted me to list all the holidays. He wouldn't be content with just the next. "St. Patrick's Day," I'd say.

"And then what Mommy, then what?"

"Your father's birthday, Easter, Mother's Day, Father's Day, 4th of July, your birthday, your brother's birthday, Mommy's birthday, Halloween, Thanksgiving, Hanukkah," and finally the one he'd wait for, "Christmas." Then he'd say, "Again, again."

"St. Patrick's Day is next," I said, bracing myself for the marathon, but he stared beyond me as if he saw something, started to speak, then stopped. "What?" I said.

"Nothing, never mind."

I walked away feeling confused, but also like I escaped.

When I replay this memory, the groove deep from the familiar needle, my son's high-pitched voice asks me: "What comes next Mommy?" and I whisper, "You die."

Catching Up

I.

I watch Desmond eat an apple whole,
front teeth piercing the red skin
and sweet white meat.

I like the skin, he says.
Riley liked the meat.

II.

He wears the same shoe size
his brother did at six, though he's only four.

Why are his feet in such a hurry?

III.

When I look at him,
it's like seeing everything
just before nothing.

What We Carry

On Riley's first day of school,
I carried his baby brother
in a sack strapped over my chest,
his blue eyes peeking out
of a blue blanket.

Mothers smiled
and approached us,
cupped his bald head
with their open hands.

Now, I carry my dead son
on my back, his arms
wrapped around my neck.

Mothers look past us,
expressionless, their hands
compressed in pockets
or under folded arms.

When Riley was alive,
I couldn't carry him anymore.
It hurt my back.

Lucky for my spine,
death doesn't weigh in pounds.

What Remains

This first anniversary of Riley's death,
I think of what remains:

photographs, the orange cast
from his broken arm, clothes

and toys, the memories fading
from my brain's circuitry,

like lost balloons, then dreams
or pure imagination.

What remains: the setting, props,
costumes, photographs of a boy,

an ephemeral few
will remember.

Proof of everything.
Proof of nothing.

IV

My Friend from Another Life

She sits across from me, wearing a purple sundress, her dark hair relaxed around her face.

"You look really great," she says, her voice thick with surprise, her eyes approving as they scan me from head to coral-painted toenails. I hear what she's left out, "compared to a year ago," the last time we had lunch together at this restaurant, shortly after Riley died.

She scooted away after that, one email at a time: "If you ever need to talk, call me," then two months of radio silence. Then lunch plans initiated by me and canceled by her. One after another, each excuse more feeble. Finally, an email from me asking how she was, because I hadn't seen her in so long. "I've never been happier. My life has never been better," she replied. I couldn't help filling in the blanks...*since your son died and you're not in my life*. Then, the kicker email, where she asked if I was *lighter these days*. I couldn't respond. How could I say I didn't want to be lighter? That without the grief's weight, I'd be nothing, and so would Riley—how could I say I wear my dead son proudly like a pregnant belly? I want to ask her if she'd be lighter without her daughter.

"You look great too," I say, "I like your dress."

"It's old," she says, "So, I don't feel good in it."

We trade awkward pauses and polite questions. I'm distracted by the bugs that accompany the creek-side view. Two land in my tea, one in my water. She notices and comments there are none in hers, says I manifest them. I think about trying to manifest them in my house. I wonder if she thinks I manifested my son's AVM, his brain hemorrhage and his death. I wonder where the line gets drawn with this manifestation thing. I wonder why we're having lunch. Closure, or starting over? Her guilt or my curiosity? Nostalgia for a time when two women became friends over pre-school chauffeuring because it was easy? A time when conversation flowed lightly. A time when both our children were alive, and we had that in common.

Vanilla Milk

Today, when I walked by the lab
where you had your blood tested
all those times, I saw our ghosts,
sitting side by side,
looking at the book about dinosaurs.

You chewed your Spider-Man shirt collar,
and I read aloud
about the barosaurus and triceratops.
You stopped me at the pliosaur,
who could swallow a person whole.
What's extinct mean? you asked.

It wasn't the best book for a child
who had almost died.

I got one thing right that day.
I remembered to bring
your vanilla milk in a box.
When the nurse came in,
I handed it to you,
told you to wait until I said *when*.

You never noticed the needle go in:
you sucked steadily through the straw,
your brown eyes glued
to the picture of the pliosaur
in the open book,

and when I said it was time to go,
you asked in your sweet,
soft voice,

Already, Mommy?

Super Boy

There can't be anything wrong with Desmond. He has to be perfectly healthy, like his favorite superheroes. He's all we have now. The whole weight of our love hangs on him. I know he feels it when we hover, checking his temperature, asking if he's hungry, examining his skin for blemishes. He sees it when we look at him in awe, fear, or gratitude he's still alive.

Our love oozes from him in spontaneous displays. A kiss on my kneecap while I wash the dishes, one on his dad's back while he works on the computer. A kiss on his teacher's hand after she watches him ride his bike, a hug for the pizza delivery guy.

I wait by his bed for him to fall asleep, his Pillow Pet lights the ceiling with blue stars and a giraffe. He tucks all five Softies in before he'll sleep. He wiggles, rolls, and burrows his head into the pillow. I know he's going to want more water, to go to the bathroom, and give me more kisses and hugs. He will want to say goodnight to his daddy again.

He rolls onto his back, blue eyes looking up at me.

"Mommy, I just love you. I really love you."

"I love you too, sweetie," I say.

"Why do you always say I love you when I say I love you?"

"I don't know," I say, "Because I do."

"I don't want you to say it too," he says. "Okay?"

"I love you, Mommy."

"Thank you," I say.

"Why did you say thank you?"

"I don't know. It seems like a nice thing to say when someone says they love you and you can't say it back."

He looks at the stars on his ceiling, then at me. "How about when I say I love you, you give me a kiss on my cheek after? Okay? How about that?"

"Okay," I say.

"Mommy, I love you."

My shadow hangs above his bed, overlapping the mural of a wall-size giraffe. His body looks peaceful, but his eyes squeeze shut.

God as a Waiter

A friend tells me
I need to ask God
for a baby.
*He will give you
one, if you ask.*

She tells me this
as if I wanted
soup or coffee.

Place the order,
Thou shall receive.

I picture God,
the tuxedoed Waiter
of all waiters, taking
our orders, ringing the bell,
serving us soup du jour.

The last thing I ordered from Him,
I never received.
He stood at my table
in His white button-down shirt,
black pants and white apron,
pulled out His order pad,
clicked His pen, and said,
*Sorry, but what you ordered
has been eighty-sixed,
we're all out of
Saving a Dying Child today.*

I nod and tell my friend
I will ask God for a baby.

She says, *Oh, by the way–
you have to believe.*

July 28th, 2012

It's Riley's second birthday,
without us.
He would have been
eight.
Instead of dead.
Instead of chalk dust.
Instead of oysterless chips of pearls.
Instead of a giant,
insatiable pit.
Instead of a collage of photos
and cutout red crayoned hearts.
Instead of our tears.
Instead of a vanilla birthday cake
bejeweled with his name.
Instead of a ghost,
haunted by us.
Instead of frozen
at six and a half.
Instead of this fucking poem.

*I Read Somewhere Only Ten Percent of Marriages Survive
the Death of a Child*

How is your marriage? my friend asks,
like it's ailing, our son's death its cancer.
Malignant cells of grief replacing
once hearty tissue. I don't know
how to respond, every reassurance
I consider sounding trite and untrue.
I remember how I used to view
our marriage, a refuge I've learned
was illusion. Hope's for the unknown,
the nursery mural painted,
a happy giraffe overlooking the crib.
I don't answer her question.
I say, *We're trying to get pregnant.*

Heaven

I can't stop looking at the broken light
above the vacant space
where Riley's bed was.
It keeps *skipping*, as Desmond
calls it, its glow like a stone
leaping smooth water before vanishing.
I'm telling him a bedtime story,
about Smiley Brewster and his cat,
Prakta, (a.k.a. Riley Brenner and Chakra),
how he blasted off in a rocket
and landed in another galaxy.
He woke not knowing where
there was, though tall vanilla milks
surrounded him and Christmas
never ended. When he asks Prakta
where they are, she meows twice.
I whisper *heaven* into Desmond's ear,
and he repeats its two soft syllables
to the manmade stars on the ceiling.
Riley didn't see me be a big boy, he says.
I see his big boy grief
shimmering like an aura over his body,
its unstoppable growth.

Somethin' New Is Brewin'

While eating at a breakfast place we used to go to before Riley died, we brainstorm names we'd choose if we had another baby. Lee proposes, "How about Riley if it's girl, Riley Two." My husband's eyes alight, his lips on the verge of turning up. He butters his toast, globbing it on, reminding me how Riley used to eat it straight from its foil wrapper, kissing it and exclaiming, "I love you so much, I want to marry you, butter!" to the shiny treasure packet of animal fat.

A framed ad for Folgers, *Somethin New Is Brewin*, adorns our booth, under which Desmond stands on the bench he should be sitting on, yelling to a waiter, "Hay is for horses! Hay is for horses!" His curly blond hair bouncing as he bops to his chanting. I know he won't eat until he gets the guy's attention.

"Riley Two? So, whad'ya think?" Lee persists.

My laugh sounds like a hiccup, as the coffee sprays from my mouth across my omelet. "That's really creepy," I say.

"You think so?" he asks. We both laugh.

"Come to think of it, maybe we should just stay away from *R* names altogether? We haven't had much luck with them. There's your father, Richard, dead, your brother, Richard, also, dead, and my Aunt Rene, who died at birth. Just think, if my parents hadn't had a second baby to make up for Rene, neither my father or I would exist, either. Or Riley." I look back at the sign, *Somethin' New Is Brewin'*. Lee notices and says, "I sure hope so."

The Unlearning

My son built a rocket today
from blocks, chairs, and toy fruit.
He showed a classmate how to flip
the power switch
(invisible to me)
to prepare for take off.
I watched from my world,
bound by facts and limitations
I'd been taught,
unable to see beyond
the room enclosing me;
while he blasted off
and soared through space,
open to infinite possibilities
it will take him
years to unlearn.

The Perfect Kiss

I walk through my house,
picking up fragments of our lives,
an arm here, an ear there.
Desmond charges me like a football player,
slowing before impact to a hummingbird's hover,
pressing gentle lips on my kneecap, his two small
hands holding my leg in place.
My focus shifts,
transcending the day's worry and minutia,
and I'm reminded by my two-year-old of Love,
stripped of the body I think I need,
to the essence of who I am . . .
I aspire to kiss so freely.

His Heart Takes Flight

Why don't I ever get to fly? Riley asked,
looking out the open window,

craning his neck skyward
like a stranded white heron.

We didn't want to tell him
about his brain's weak vessels,

*You just don't know
what makes these things bleed,* the doctor warned.

I told him,
Someday, you'll fly.

While he slept,
the vessels gave way.

Today, his heart is flying to Canada,
a piece of him taking off,

soaring over the Golden Gate Bridge,
Mount Rainier, eternal bodies of water,

landing in Vancouver, somewhere
I've never been.

I imagine the girl
who will inherit his heart

in a white lace nightgown,
her small body supine

on a feather bed,
her mother gazing skyward,

palm on her daughter's chest
like a prayer.

Family Photos

Acknowledgments

Grateful acknowledgment is made to the editors of the following publications in which these poems, or previous versions, first appeared:

Broad!: "Choices," "Mothering My Son's Dead Brother"

Cultural Weekly: "God as a Waiter," "I Have 2x the Love For 1 Child," "Knowing," "Mothering a Dead Child," "What Would Wislawa Szymborska Do?"

Diverse Voices Quarterly: "Where the World Ends"

Foliate Oak: "Happy Hour" (originally titled "The Neglected Vow")," "Riley Died Again Yesterday," "The Perfect Kiss"

Forge: "Something Else"

L.K. Thayer's Poetry Juice Bar: "Blindsided" (originally titled "Fool's Gold")

Madeline Sharples' Choices: "My Friend From Another Life"

Memoirs Ink: "Riley Day"

Poet Lore: "Into the Schoolyard"

The Coachella Review: "Your Permanent Tooth"

The Write Place at the Write Time: "July 28th, 2012," "Out of Body," "Shifting Sand," "Vanilla Milk"

Thank you to Alexis Rhone Fancher, Tresha Haefner, April Ossman, Pamela Schwab, Marilyn Conrad, Joy Dabby, Mary Beth DeLucia, Chuck Gardner, Ella Gorham, Bambi Here, Baz Here, Judi Kaufman, Roz Levine, Juanita Beth Morgan, Julie Sharp, Madeline Sharples, and Carolyn Ziel. Thank you to Jack Grapes and all my Wednesday-morning comrades for the inspiration, and for providing a nurturing space to first share these poems. Also, thank you to my friends and family who supported me by reading these poems. Thank you to my husband Lee for your unwavering support, and for being by my side through everything. Thank you to my son Desmond for continuing to bring joy into our lives.

About the Author

Chanel Brenner's poems have appeared in *Cultural Weekly*, *Poet Lore*, *Rattle*, *The Coachella Review*, *Diverse Voices Quarterly*, *Foliate Oak*, *Glassworks*, and others. She was awarded first prize for her poetry in The Write Place At the Write Time's contest. She lives in Los Angeles with her husband and son.